CW00456114

Christmas Eve

Daniel Kehlmann was born in Munich in 1975 and lives in Berlin and New York. His novels and plays have won numerous prizes, including the Candide Prize, the Doderer Prize, the Kleist Prize, the Welt Literature Prize and the Thomas Mann Prize. His novel *Measuring the World* has been translated into more than forty languages and is one of the greatest successes of post-war German literature. His play *The Mentor* premiered in the English language at the Ustinov Theatre, Bath, translated by Christopher Hampton and transferred to London's West End. He is currently teaching at New York University.

Christopher Hampton was born in the Azores in 1946. He wrote his first play, *When Did You Last See My Mother?*, at the age of eighteen. Since then, his plays have included *The Philanthropist*, *Savages*, *Tales from Hollywood*, *Les Liaisons Dangereuses*, *White Chameleon*, *The Talking Cure* and *Appomattox*. He has translated plays by Ibsen, Molière, von Horváth, Chekhov, Florian Zeller, Yasmina Reza (including '*Art*', *Life* × *3*, and *The God of Carnage*) and Daniel Kehlmann. His television work includes adaptations of *The History Man* and *Hotel du Lac*. His screenplays include *The Honorary Consul*, *The Good Father*, *Dangerous Liaisons*, *Mary Reilly*, *Total Eclipse*, *The Quiet American*, *Atonement*, *Cheri*, *A Dangerous Method*, *Carrington*, *The Secret Agent* and *Imagining Argentina*, the last three of which he also directed.

DANIEL KEHLMANN

Christmas Eve

a play for two actors and a clock

translated by
CHRISTOPHER HAMPTON

FABER & FABER

First published in 2017
by Faber and Faber Limited
74–77 Great Russell Street, London WC1B 3DA

Typeset by Country Setting, Kingsdown, Kent CT14 8ES
Printed and bound by CPI Group (UK) Ltd, Croydon, CR0 4YY

A CIP record for this book is available from the British Library

ISBN 978-0-571-34525-0

Christmas Eve, in this translation by Christopher Hampton, was commissioned by the Ustinov Studio, Theatre Royal Bath, and first presented on 19 October 2017. The cast was as follows:

Thomas Patrick Baladi
Judith Niamh Cusack

Director Laurence Boswell
Designer Tim Shortall
Lighting Designer Colin Grenfell
Sound Designer and Composer   Jon Nicholls
Casting Director Ginny Schiller

As *Heilig Abend* the play had its first production in German at the Theater in der Josefstadt, Vienna, on 2 February 2017.

Characters

Thomas
Judith

CHRISTMAS EVE

The time shown on the wall clock at the beginning of the play – as well as whenever specific times are referred to in the dialogue – should conform appropriately. What's essential is that as the last words are spoken the hands reach midnight.

The symbol / signifies that one character begins to speak while the other is still talking, interrupting.

A plainly furnished room: two chairs and a table. There are papers on the table, as well as a Thermos flask and paper cups, plus a tiny Santa Claus and an old-fashioned telephone with a cord. On the wall, clearly readable, a clock is hanging. It's 10:30.

Thomas sits behind the table and waits, motionless. The door opens and a woman, Judith, walks in. The door is immediately closed behind her.

Thomas Coffee? Cigarette, perhaps? I know you don't smoke. But if you ever felt like making an exception, as you sometimes do, now would be a good moment. Where were you yesterday evening?

He waits. She doesn't answer. She looks shocked and confused.

'As you sometimes do,' you're thinking. Why does he say, 'As you sometimes do'? I hardly ever smoke, how does he know I sometimes do?

Pause.

So yesterday afternoon and evening, where were you?

Pause.

You were at home. I know that. Who else was there? Please sit down.

His tone suddenly becomes commanding.

Sit down!

She does so.

Who else was there?

3

Pause.

Your husband was there. I know that.

Judith My husband . . . ?

Thomas Your ex-husband. I know. Who else?

Judith What?

Thomas Who else was with you?

Judith Nobody.

Thomas I know. What did you do?

He waits, she says nothing.

What did you do?

Judith I don't understand.

Thomas You and your ex-husband. Two-thirty in the afternoon till eleven at night, that's a long stint. 10:52, to be precise. That's when he left. Not that late. The night was still young. Isn't that what they say? 'The night is still young.' So what did you do?

Judith What did we do?

Thomas We don't have a tremendous amount of time, so I'd be obliged if you could answer a bit more expeditiously. What were you doing? Did you have something to eat, for example?

Judith Maybe.

Thomas Maybe?

Judith I can't remember!

Thomas You can't remember?

Judith I don't think so. I don't think we had anything to eat.

Thomas What about a drink?

Judith Probably. Is there a law against it?

Thomas Anything alcoholic?

Judith Is there a law against it?

Thomas Depends on the circumstances. For example, if you went on to drive . . .

Judith I don't even have a licence!

Thomas Driving without a licence really is against the law.

Judith I didn't drive!

Thomas Good. You see? If we start talking to each other, we can clear up all sorts of issues. Was there much?

Judith Much what?

Thomas Alcohol. Yesterday evening. You and your ex-husband, between two-thirty in the afternoon and 10:52 in the evening, did you drink much?

Judith No!

Thomas Good. Drinking in moderation is better for the health.

Judith What do you want from me?

Thomas To find out what went wrong.

Judith When? Where?

Thomas Yesterday. Today. Now. Shortly. If you'd be so kind as to answer expeditiously.

Judith You've just hauled me out of a taxi.

Thomas Just?

Judith An hour ago / and it was . . .

Thomas Twenty-six minutes.

Judith Yes, and . . .

Thomas If you wanted to round it up, you could say half an hour ago. An hour ago is simply wrong.

He points at the clock. It's 10:35.

You could say it's 10:38. Or you could say it's coming up to eleven, if you didn't feel like being too exact. But what you couldn't say is it's ten. It's past 10:30, we're closer to eleven than ten. Please be precise.

Judith All right, I'll be precise. First I thought it must be some drunk, but then there was a second car and a third one behind me, they forced us to stop. Then there were two men, one of whom held an ID card up against the window, which he pocketed right away and refused to show again. 'Get out,' they said. 'Now!' I was so taken by surprise, I just got out. Then I sat between them in this car and they didn't say a word, and whenever I asked them something, they pretended not to hear, and now I'm here, wherever this is, they took away my telephone and I don't know where I am. May I ask what's going on?

Thomas Wine?

Judith What?

Thomas Was it wine you drank yesterday evening?

Judith Probably.

Thomas You see, that's the way forward. That's how we'll make some progress. Did you get round to having sex?

Judith You have no right . . .!

Thomas Just curious.

Judith This is incredible –

Thomas You don't have to answer. It's not essential. It has no bearing on our subject. Did you get round to having sex?

Pause. Judith is staggered.

For old times' sake? I can imagine the scene. Getting late, after a few glasses of wine, expensive wine, I dare say . . .

Judith No!

Thomas No, in the sense of refusing to answer the question? Or in the sense of you didn't get round to having sex? Or in the sense of the wine wasn't that expensive?

Judith Needless to say, in the sense of refusing to answer the question.

Thomas I understand. You could also simply have said, no, we didn't get round to having sex. Which would have been the correct answer. So, once again . . .

Judith Where are we?

Thomas Yesterday evening . . .

Judith Are you even a policeman?

Thomas Where were you?

Pause.

Judith At home.

Thomas Who was with you?

Judith My divorced husband.

Thomas Why?

Judith Why?

Thomas Yes, why? You get a divorce, he keeps coming round, why?

Judith He comes to see me sometimes.

Thomas Are you friends?

Judith Yes.

Thomas I know it's theoretically possible, but is it really? It's not possible for me. Not with my ex-wife! We don't go and see each other. We don't drink wine together, not even cheap wine. She calls me the biggest mistake of her life. She says I'm a nasty piece of work. A bad person. She says I stole her youth away. It's understandable she would say that in the last years of our marriage, but that was five years ago and she's still saying it. My appearance makes her suicidal. The sound of my voice brings instant misery. She says my existence has ruined her faith in the human race.

Judith Who does she say that to?

Thomas Anyone who asks. And to quite a lot of people who don't ask. She even says it when she's alone.

Judith When she's alone?

Thomas She thinks I can hear her. She thinks I've installed microphones in her flat.

Judith And have you?

Thomas Please!

Judith But if you haven't installed microphones . . .

Thomas I know, because our daughter's told me! I don't use microphones for personal reasons. It's not allowed.

Judith Oh, not allowed.

Thomas This is still a law-abiding country.

Judith Ah.

Thomas Your friends still haven't managed to put a stop to that.

8

Judith What friends?

Thomas Precisely. What friends? That's what we need to discuss. That's what I want to hear more about.

Judith Could be your wife is right.

Pause. It takes him a minute to understand.

Thomas Think that's a good idea? To antagonise me?

Judith I don't want to antagonise you.

Thomas But you want to show me that you're not going to let yourself be intimidated.

Judith I don't want to show you anything, I want to get out of here.

Thomas I think you do want to show me something.

Judith I couldn't care less about you.

Thomas Hard to believe.

Judith I care about you the way I might care about a rock dropping on my head. It's tremendously unpleasant, it might even kill me, but that doesn't make it interesting.

Thomas I shouldn't have mentioned my wife. Now you think you can treat me how you like.

Judith You mean your ex-wife. Please be precise.

Thomas People like you, as soon as you find out something about a person, you'll turn it against them. Your hatred justifies everything.

Judith My hatred?

Thomas Of the state. Of the rules. In other words, of me.

Judith Will you just tell me why I'm here?! Am I a witness or have I been arrested? Can I make a phone call? / I know my rights.

Thomas I'm as reluctant to be here as you are. It's Christmas! I could be at home.

Judith With your daughter?

Thomas No.

Judith Because your daughter's with your ex-wife?

Thomas What about you? Where should you have been at a quarter to eleven on Christmas Eve? If we hadn't hauled you out of your car, where would you be now?

Judith I'm sure you know the answer to that as well.

Thomas Do we really exist?

Judith What?

Thomas What do philosophers talk about among themselves? Do they discuss whether we really exist? Seriously: do we exist?

Judith I shouldn't worry about that if I were you.

Thomas I exist, that's hard to deny, but I could have dreamed the world. You could be part of my dream. This clock, this chair, do they actually exist?

Judith We'd have to reach back a long way, but the short answer is yes.

Thomas So that's your professional opinion? As an occupant of a Chair in Philosophy, you certify that I exist?

Judith I'm not saying another word, until you explain to me why I'm here!

Thomas Calm down. I'm not doing anything to you. Not yet anyway. And you're right, of course I know where you were headed. To your parents' lovely house. The villa with the garden and the fitted carpets and the Alsatian. Hasso? Bello?

Judith Henry.

Thomas Henry, yes. Good food, discreet music, a beautifully decorated tree all the way up to the ceiling. Perhaps even a spot of carol singing. Wouldn't do me any good. But last year you spent Christmas with your parents as well, and the year before and the year before that.

Judith How do you know where I was the year before last?

Thomas We've been able to check where your telephone has been, every minute since you bought it. Before that you had a different phone. We could also check where that was. Why do you go to your parents for Christmas? You were always running away from there! Again and again, away from that beautiful house, always as far away as you could get. I don't think you're even very fond of the dog.

Judith I'm not saying another word, until you explain to me / why I'm here. I want –

Thomas You already said that, but you won't stick to it. You like the sound of your own voice too much. Occupational hazard. Anyway, your poor parents must be wondering where you are. It's almost midnight. Shall we give them a call?

Slowly, he pushes the phone over to her. She stares at it, but makes no move. She's struggling with herself, it's a difficult decision.

Judith No.

Thomas But they're waiting for you. In the beautiful house with the fitted carpets and Henry, they'll be worrying.

Judith No.

Thomas Are you that embarrassed to be here? So embarrassed you'd rather your parents were worrying than finding out where you are. Reconsider. Think of those two poor old farts.

She doesn't move. He draws the phone back away from her.

You're a proper scourge of the bourgeoisie.

Judith Can you talk in anything but clichés?

Thomas Clichés are underestimated, clichés are very useful. Tell me, how did your parents and your husband – when he was still your husband – how did they get on? You were a glamorous couple, you with your long hair, him with his full beard. Then your year in Bolivia. You called three times! Only three times! Was that thoughtful? Then two months in Chile when you didn't phone at all.

Judith How can you know that? You can't possibly know how often I called. Even with the best technology you couldn't / know that. At the time, I didn't even have a mobile.

Thomas It's a very interesting subject, but time is pressing, so let's just say there are several ways we can find out something like that. For example, we can pull the phone records for your parents' house for the last twenty-four years; but we could also phone up your mother, tell her we're working for a university magazine and writing an article about you.

Judith She would have told me.

Thomas Not if we said the article was a birthday surprise, mothers love that kind of thing, mothers are crazy about birthday surprises.

Judith We were in Bolivia, but we were never in Chile. There's a lot you don't know.

Thomas You travelled into Chile on false passports. If you knew how much we can find out, when we're interested in somebody. Mind you, those are only facts. Facts are blind. A fact can mean one thing or mean something altogether different. What I find much more interesting is: did your husband and your parents get on? I suspect it was pretty tense every time they met, the conversation was strained. The professor of dead languages, your father, would have made a remark, then your husband would have said something, then your father again, and so on and so on. About Cuba or Northern Ireland . . . or Israel!

Judith Who's told you that?

Thomas You just need a bit of imagination. And I can easily imagine how much your parents worried about you. Their only child. So talented. Whatever you did, everyone always piped up: 'What a talented child!' Riding lessons, piano lessons, fencing lessons, singing lessons, the private school, the Cambridge college, think how much it all cost! And what thanks did they get? Three phone calls from Bolivia. And silence from Chile. Unreliable friends, drugs, parties, pamphlets full of grammatical errors.

Judith Grammatical errors?

Thomas Nothing wrong with that, everyone makes grammatical errors.

Judith I can imagine that you do, but I don't.

Thomas Everyone does –

Judith Show me one.

Thomas We're short of time. Just take my word for it. I know all your essays. You'll never find a more faithful reader. I even read your doctoral thesis about Frantz . . . Fan . . .

Judith Frantz Fanon.

Thomas Yes, with a 'tz'. Who spells Frantz with a 'tz'?

Judith You read that?

Thomas I did, I did. I went to great lengths to pass it along to a colleague, but you'd be amazed what ingenious excuses people make to get out of reading 764 pages of *Frantz Fanon's Concept of Revolutionary Violence*. And they only gave me a day.

Judith Was it rough?

Thomas Spare me your arrogance. It was boring: not complicated, not difficult to understand, just boring. You and Mr Fanon getting worked up about the rich and the poor, as if the difference between them had never occurred to anyone else. You'd like the world to be a better place: who wouldn't?

Judith Fanon deals with colonialism and the rights of the oppressed –

Thomas – to resort to violence.

Judith Yes.

Thomas To violence!

Judith Yes.

Thomas There we have it. The big word. Violence. That's probably why you wanted to go to South America. You could equally have gone to Africa, but I'll admit, Bolivia has better music and, no doubt, better parties. The Wretched of the Earth. Did you really find them? In Bolivia?

Judith To find the Wretched of the Earth, all you need to do is walk down any street in this city. Step into any supermarket.

Thomas Have you any idea, Professor, what I have to deal with every day? All the cretinous jihadis I have to keep an eye on, all the frustrated losers who can't find a girlfriend and announce on the net they're going to fight for Allah – and quite honestly, all you can hope is that they'll do it and get themselves shot somewhere in the desert, before they drive a truck into a crowd or start laying about them with a knife on some bridge. The truth is, we're completely powerless against people who are prepared to die. The man who's prepared to die is unconquerable, unstoppable, immune from any punishment, only you can't say that in public, because people are scared enough as it is. Those murderers in Paris, are those your Wretched of the Earth? Your sort really is the last thing I need. All those old theories. The day before yesterday's world. Dusty ghosts from your history seminars. When we stumbled on you, we had to laugh. My colleague said: 'Does this sort of thing really still go on?'

Judith Now that oppression's been abolished and poverty done away with, you mean.

Thomas I'd prefer it as well, a fairer distribution of wealth. Firstly in my direction and then to everyone else. Banks are corrupt and governments are venal, I know that as well as you do. Possibly better than you.

Judith The cretinous jihadis, as you call them, are just a big diversion. They're an excuse to limit everyone's freedom. They're an excuse to call anyone who doesn't support the status quo a suspect. The fact is, they support the system they believe they're fighting.

Thomas Support the system? Unlike you, Professor, I have to watch certain videos that invade my dreams every night. Every day I have to imagine what might happen if we were to underestimate a single one of them. A big diversion! Be careful what you say or I might lose my sense of humour!

Judith I think you already have.

Thomas The system may be bad, but –

Judith – it's still the best we've got. I think I've heard that profound, witty and original thought quite often enough.

Thomas Perhaps it's true.

Judith Suppose it *isn't* true. What if it *isn't* the best system? What if it's really a cruel system which exploits people and keeps them fearful and ignorant and which is at this moment turning its back on even the semblance of democracy, what then?

Thomas I can't imagine a better system.

Judith I can believe that, but what does that prove? Only that *you* can't imagine a better system!

Thomas You're assuming I'm immune to being insulted and you're right to some extent, but only to some extent. 'Structural violence as opposed to revolutionary violence': when I look at that strand of your stuff, it's like drowning in the seventies.

Judith It was true then and it's true today. It's just not fashionable any more.

Thomas Clearly it is. Last year they gave you a university Chair.

Judith And the fact the state tolerates me puts me in the wrong?

Thomas The fact it pays you. Yes, that does a bit. I think it puts you in the wrong.

Judith It shows how kind and generous the state is.

Thomas Isn't it?

Judith Don't worry, it's paying out less and less, and in a few years they'll be turning out nothing but people who want no more out of life than miniature phones and slimline laptops.

Thomas What do you have against slimline laptops?

Judith Nothing, they're very handy. Secular miracles. How marvellously slim they've become! And they're going to get even slimmer! A glorious future.

Thomas If a tree falls in the forest and nobody sees it fall, does it really fall?

Judith What?

Thomas As long as you're here. A philosopher. I've always wanted to know. If a tree falls in the forest and no one's there, does it really fall?

Judith Who's asking the question?

Thomas Who's asking the question?

Judith Yes, who's asking the question?

Thomas Well, I am.

Judith Do you see?

Thomas No.

Judith Just think about it!

Thomas But –

Judith Come to my seminar. Maybe we can help you.

Thomas But which one? 'Terminology 1', Monday two to four, or 'An Introduction to Political Philosophy', Wednesday five to seven? This term it's 'Historical Theories of Structural Violence'. Yes, perhaps I should come. Perhaps I might finally understand what 'structural violence' means. But I'm more interested in the thing about the tree.

Judith You have no intention of finding out what structural violence is.

Thomas I admit we're a bit short of time.

Judith It's when you teach someone that the differences between rich and poor are natural, as permanently ordained as the sequence of the stars. When you teach someone he's free, because he's able to buy the latest phone, so he can spread the news about what songs and films he's streamed.

Thomas What is it you have against these gadgets?

Judith It's when someone is given no opportunity to learn, but he's told he can be whatever he wants to be, as long as he thinks positively. And it's when he's talked into believing that if he's not happy, it's his fault. If he's not happy, he hasn't been thinking positively enough and all the bad things that are happening to him serve him right.

Thomas And that's when he reaches for his gun or his knife?

Judith No. A very few of them reach for a knife. Hardly any of them reach for a submachine gun.

Thomas So the cretinous jihadis are our own invention?

Judith They're real and they're sub-human, but there are very few of them and it's as if they were invented for the benefit of a system that is actually invulnerable, but wants to claim it's under threat.

Thomas The danger isn't real?

Judith Traffic accidents are more dangerous.

Thomas Traffic accidents are accidents, not violence!

Judith Not violence? Companies spend millions to persuade you you must have a car that can reach a speed our brain is not equipped to handle; and on top of that they persuade you you have to go into debt to pay for it. And that's not violence?

Thomas No.

Judith Twenty-five thousand dead in Europe, last year. Not violence?

Thomas No, not violence.

Judith And my being here, that's not violence either?

Thomas No, it's a request. A request for information. We respect any opinion, however stupid it is, we'll defend the right to hold it. We fight for the right of the law-abiding citizen to stand up for absolutely any idea, however nonsensical.

Judith Law-abiding citizens. That's downright touching.

Thomas Yes, those who abide by the laws of our state.

Judith Why am I here?

Thomas You know very well.

Judith I have no idea.

Thomas I don't believe you.

Judith It's your duty to tell me why I'm here!

Thomas How do you know what my duty is? Off the TV?

Judith What's your name? You have to give me your service number.

Thomas Promise you, I would if I had one.

Judith Who are you?

Thomas And who are you?

Judith What?

Thomas I thought it was some kind of a philosophical question. Who am I, who are you, where do we come from, where are we going. Do you kill people?

Pause.

Judith I beg your pardon.

Thomas 'Like the spear of Achilles, violence heals the wounds it creates.' Sartre. In his preface to the book by Frantz-with-a-tz Fanon. Do you kill people?

Judith Do I . . .?

Thomas 'Violence heals the wounds it creates.' Or are you just an armchair radical? Are you one of them? I don't think you are.

Judith You can't charge me for what I'm thinking.

Thomas But I can charge you for what you do.

Judith And you would maintain that an opinion is a kind of action. If I put it about that the system deserves to be attacked, you would maintain I'd be guilty, if anyone who heard what I'd said decided to –

Thomas An opinion is not an action. An opinion is an opinion. An action is an action.

He picks up a piece of paper and reads aloud.

'We claim responsibility for this action, carried out at midnight on the 24th of December. We claim responsibility for taking necessary and drastic measures to destabilise the status quo. We claim responsibility for resorting to any means to call into question any situation alleged to have no alternative.'

He breaks off and looks at the clock.

'State rhetoric about protecting the innocent benefits a system that has taken pains to bring about a state of affairs in which there are as few innocents as there are genuinely guilty. There are no longer any combatants, only prisoners of necessity. Whoever calls for compassion is calling for the struggle to be abandoned. Whoever wishes to continue the struggle accepts that they will be labelled enemies of humanity.' From your laptop. A very slim model, by the way. Very fast, very good screen.

Judith That's not been published.

Thomas No.

Judith The computer's never been online.

Thomas How so? That's most unusual.

Judith It's never been connected to the internet.

Thomas Never?

Judith Not once.

Thomas Why's that? So that the contents of its hard drive remain absolutely secure and secret? A computer that's never been connected to the internet. It shouldn't surprise you if that makes us curious.

Judith There's no law against writing something like that!

Thomas Of course not.

Judith But?

Thomas But nothing.

Judith Then why am I here?

Pause.

Thomas Where's the bomb?

Pause.

Very nice. Bit of conversation, getting to know one another a bit. But now we need to get down to business.

Judith What bomb?

Thomas We don't have much time and you keep saying 'what?' And 'how?' And 'I beg your pardon' and are constantly amazed, when all I need to know are some extremely simple facts. 'We claim responsibility for this action, carried out at midnight on the 24th of December.' Something very straightforward for once. We have just under an hour and I'd really like to know: where's the bomb?

Judith There is no bomb!

Thomas You write about the struggle. You write about victims, you write about the regrettable threat to innocent bystanders, you write about accepting the inevitability of being labelled enemies of humanity.

Judith It's for my seminar! What would a statement look like that claimed responsibility for a drastic initiative –

Thomas A terror attack!

Judith – if it were to have a solid theoretical foundation. For my seminar! You haven't arrested me for that?

Thomas We haven't arrested you.

Judith Are you saying I haven't been / arrested?

Thomas As you correctly emphasise, it is not illegal to write bollocks on your own computer. We're simply concerned, and we've invited you to visit us. Which you've very kindly agreed to do.

Judith I could have said no?

Thomas People can always say no.

Judith I didn't have to come? Down there on the street I could have said: 'Fuck off, I'm driving on'?

Thomas Did anyone read you your rights? You watch TV. If no one reads you your rights, you're not under arrest.

Judith So I can go?

Thomas If you're not under arrest, you're free to go.

Judith Now?

Thomas I'd be grateful if you stayed.

She gets up, goes over to the door and tries to open it. It's locked.

Judith Open the door.

Thomas By all means.

He doesn't move.

Judith Am I under arrest?

Thomas No.

Judith Then open the door.

Thomas Here's the thing. We invited you in for a conversation and you came along. We appreciate that. / But –

Judith Open the door!

Thomas – if you were to break off the conversation precisely at the question: 'Where's the bomb?', that would mean we'd be obliged to take certain measures. As you can see, time's marching on. The 24th of December. Midnight.

Judith If I'm not under arrest, you have to / let me go.

Thomas *If* you're not under arrest.

Judith You said I wasn't . . .

Thomas Not yet.

Judith Do you mean I'm not under arrest, as long as I stay here of my own free will. Whereas if I decide to go . . .

Thomas We'll have to arrest you.

Judith Then do it.

Thomas Wouldn't be a good idea. For any of us. In court, it looks much better if you've been co-operative.

Judith Arrest me or let me go! We live in a democracy. Not all the rules have been suspended.

Thomas In the face of a definite threat, we have considerable powers. Because of you, a whole lot of people have been called away from their Christmas tree. Every one of whom would rather be with their family.

Judith All because of me?

Thomas All because of you, since this afternoon. At five o'clock we cracked your password, by 5:30 we'd accessed the text from your hard drive, by 5:45 it had been read and the counter-terror operation had been activated.

Judith And you hauled me out of my taxi.

Thomas At eight minutes past ten. Should have gone quicker, I acknowledge that. At first somebody decided we should just put you under surveillance, then another directive was issued and we grabbed you.

Judith How did you get into my computer?

Thomas Is that the kind of question an innocent person would ask? 'How did you get into my computer?'

Judith This is all ridiculous! In –

She looks at the clock.

– thirty-two minutes you'll see that there is no bomb! Arrest me or let me go!

Pause.

Thomas Refusal to make a statement, the presence of a lawyer, to be informed of the exact charges against you, blah blah blah. Those are your rights. If you need an interpreter, one will be provided. Do you need an interpreter? You just have to say. You also have the right to inform others of your arrest. And if you like, you can have all this information in writing. That's also your right. The right to obtain your rights in writing. And now the highlight: anything you say may be taken down and used in evidence against you.

Judith Then that's what I'd like.

Thomas What?

Judith A lawyer and a phone call.

Thomas See, that's the problem with arresting people. You've hardly read them their rights . . .

Judith And I would like everything in writing.

Thomas On Christmas Eve? The secretary is in Ibiza!

Judith It's my right. I want my rights in writing.

He hesitates, then picks up the phone.

Thomas She wants the list of rights in writing . . . I don't know, isn't there some laminated . . . Oh, just write them all out!

He hangs up.

Judith I want to speak to my lawyer.

Thomas You do have a good lawyer, I know that. Dr Kregler, he's expensive, but he's a man of conviction, you can rely on him. He's in Iceland and even if you can get him on the phone, it'll be quite a time until he gets here.

Judith Then you find me a lawyer!

Thomas On Christmas Eve?

Judith It's my right. That's what you said.

Thomas It's your right, but I don't have the time. A bomb is due to explode at midnight.

Judith You'll see, at midnight, nothing is going to explode. Find me a lawyer!

Thomas We'll worry about that when we're finished here.

Judith When are we finished?

Thomas When the bomb is defused.

Judith There is no bomb!

Thomas Then you don't need a lawyer.

Judith I have a right to one.

Thomas I have rights as well. For example, to waive your rights in the case of clear and present danger.

Judith But there is no danger!

Thomas Good for you. Good for everybody not threatened with disaster. Admittedly, bad for me. But if the bomb does explode, it'll be even worse for me. We'll phone your lawyer later. You will not refuse to make a statement.

Pause. Judith is shaken, the extent of her helplessness is becoming clear to her.

You see that mirror? As you well know, a mirror like that is never just a mirror, so who's watching us?

Pause.

26

And you're wondering if what they say is true. Electric shocks, truth drugs, waterboarding.

Judith says nothing, she's really afraid now.

If you want to know whether we really do all that, just keep going the way you are, Professor. If you really want to know.

He approaches her menacingly. She holds up a hand to protect her face, expecting that she's about to be hit.

You're going to speak to me now. You're going to tell me where the bomb is. I already have enough to put you in prison for a very, very long time. So you're going to stop all the games, no more fucking bullshit. Unless you want to find out what it is we do.

Judith You probably do do all those things –

She pulls herself together. She's suddenly realised something. She sits up straight and speaks with a newly acquired strength.

– but you're not going to do them to me.

Thomas Aren't we?

Judith Foreigners, who don't speak the language and have brown skin and beards, you can treat how you like. No one gives a damn. But you can't torture me. I have a university Chair. I know people in the media. I can go on television, I can speak in very long sentences. I write articles. It's not going to work with me.

Thomas Do you know what a bomb can do to a body? There's still time to evacuate the area. In this kind of situation we have special powers.

He stands over her threateningly, but it's not working any more, Judith is unimpressed.

Judith All right, show me your special powers. Bring out the drugs. Bring on the waterboards. You can't do anything. You have all those armed men with bullet-proof vests and expensive listening devices, but the truth of the matter is you're standing around feeling helpless.

Thomas Do you really trust the system? Perhaps you shouldn't. If you're right about all the things you write about, perhaps you shouldn't. First I'd get a standard reprimand for overstepping my authority, then I'd get a medal and a promotion. That's the way it goes. Then it would be me on television and the judge would bar you from giving interviews. Judges are allowed to do that. A judge can do practically anything.

Judith Just look at me. Do I look like the kind of person who wants to murder people? You've seen murderers, do I look like one?

Thomas Murderers don't look like / murderers.

Judith They look like normal people, I know that's what they say, but is it true? It isn't really true. You don't believe that and even if you really do think I look like a murderer . . . Do I look like someone who could build a bomb? I'm an academic who writes boring stuff about structural violence and occasionally goes on a demonstration. Look at me. Down in the cellar wearing gloves, with bottles of acid and instructions off the internet? Risking blowing myself up, losing my hands, is that what I look like? You don't believe I'm capable of something like that. I don't believe you think that.

Pause.

Thomas Maybe not.

Pause.

But what about your husband?

Judith My husband?

Thomas Ex-husband. Sorry. Your ex-husband.

Judith You mean, Peter's . . .

Thomas Yes, what did you think? He's in the next room. We arrested him as he left your house yesterday evening, at 10:52, when the night was still young. He was our principal suspect. You were only just on the edge of the picture. So his interrogator has had a very long start. But we can catch up.

Judith Catch up?

Thomas Confess before he does. He can go home whenever he likes. All he has to do is incriminate you and we'll open proceedings against you. Then it becomes your bomb. And he goes free. That's the deal we've offered him. That's how the justice system works.

Judith That's ridiculous.

Thomas In almost every case, there's somebody who does a deal with us and goes home free. Didn't you know that? We don't need justice, that's what God and his angels are there for, we need a *narrative*. If he talks, we have one, and a very high-profile one. And he will talk. People will go to any lengths not to have to go to prison. And he's very tired. And luckily he's no longer your husband. Otherwise his statement would not be admissible. You were a bit hasty with the divorce. If you want to commit a crime together, stay married.

Judith What sort of a statement can he make? There is no bomb!

Thomas Last week, we found traces of explosive on his suitcase. At the airport. A swab.

Judith Anyone could have handled the suitcase. A taxi driver. A porter. Anybody. That's not proof.

Thomas You're right. That's why we don't call it proof, we call it evidence.

Judith You took a random swab / and –

Thomas Not entirely random. We were working from an incriminating statement.

Judith From whom?

Thomas Ariane. Lovely name, isn't it? She was his student and for a short time also his . . . well, you know what he's like. The old story. Him and his students. You're not married to him any more, so we can speak frankly. Anyway, Ariane somehow knew what was going on and it suddenly dawned on her that anyone who knew about something and kept their mouth shut was an accomplice, and she didn't want to go to jail for him, especially as he'd treated her really badly. You know what he's like. Then we took the swab, when Peter flew to the Sociological Conference in Frankfurt, where he gave that unbelievably interesting lecture about late capitalism's systematic peeling away from democracy. We briefly took him into custody, you should have seen him, all pale and sweaty, but then we had to let him go. Firstly because, as you so helpfully pointed out, a swab doesn't constitute proof, and secondly, we knew of course we could follow him and keep an eye on his associates, so that's what we did, good, old-fashioned police work. And his associates turned out to be you. Then your computer came to our attention and the fact it had never been online, and so yesterday we acquired the computer.

The wine delivery, do you remember? Odd fellow with three cases of wine and a delivery van who rang the bell till you came down to the street and then he tried to persuade you in a scarcely understandable accent, while you kept saying you hadn't ordered any wine and he kept waving the receipt at you and insisting the wine was yours and you kept saying you were sure it wasn't and then he had to phone somebody and then he asked you again and just as you'd really had enough, he said he was sorry and finally drove off. Seven and a half minutes. That's all the time we needed. When it comes to breaking in, we're really good, no burglar can hold a candle to us. And then we saw your announcement of an action on the 24th of December. Christmas: that could almost count as mitigating circumstances. Not so much damage caused on Christmas Day, not so many people about, the squares are empty, the department stores are closed, so are the ministries. You probably planned it that way. Great symbolic statement, probably no one killed – perfect.

Judith You listened in on us yesterday. You've definitely concealed microphones in my house.

Thomas We don't do things like that.

Judith Because of your great regard for civil rights?

Thomas Because it isn't necessary. We don't plant microphones any more. Nowadays people bring their own microphones home with them.

Judith Did we speak about an attack?

Thomas No, but what does that prove? If anything, it's even more suspicious.

Judith More suspicious, that we didn't talk about bombs?

Thomas In a way. I mean, to spend a whole evening, all those hours, without mentioning the word 'bomb'? We couldn't help noticing. Why so careful? After all, you keep writing about drastic measures. Why weren't they a topic of conversation? Except for one thing: 'It'll soon be over.' He said that and then you changed the subject. What did he mean by 'It'll soon be over'?

Judith How should I know? I have no idea. I really don't /
remember –

Thomas Of course you don't. You have no idea, but it
was enough for us. 'It'll soon be over.' We arrested him
outside your door.

Judith Arrested him outside my door?

Thomas On his way home. At 10:52.

Judith That means he's been here a whole day.

Pause.

Twenty-four hours. That means you have to let him go!

Thomas says nothing.

Or bring him in front of a judge. If you go on holding
him without a judge seeing him, nothing is admissible.
Nothing he says. You can't use any of it. And before you
ask, yes, I do know that from watching TV.

Pause.

And also because I've taken a lifelong interest in my civil
rights.

Thomas We'll call a judge as soon as you incriminate
him. The judge won't like it, because it's Christmas, but
he won't have a choice. Your statement will give us our
case. Then Peter can stay here and you can go home to
your parents.

Judith It'll be midnight soon, then you'll see that
nothing's happened.

Thomas Even if nothing happens, it doesn't change that
much. All that evidence. The swab, the laptop, your
strange manifesto claiming responsibility.

Judith It wasn't a manifesto! It was a / theoretical –

Thomas Whatever it was. Sufficient grounds to intervene. Maybe the bomb was badly designed, maybe you would have tried again. All we need is a confession that you had something planned. He has to incriminate you or you him. We've called out all these people. It can't be kept a secret. At the moment the media knows nothing, but soon things will start to trickle out. So we need a confession from somebody, a story, otherwise what's this going to look like? All these people who couldn't get back to their families. We don't like to be accused of paranoia. We need a confession.

Judith I thought this was a democracy.

Thomas So it is, that's why we need a confession.

Judith I'm not going to incriminate him and he won't incriminate me.

Thomas That's what you think. But don't underestimate human weakness. You've only been here for an hour, he's had twenty-four. Even a man as innocent as a baby will accuse someone else if he's afraid that someone else is going to accuse him. It's in our nature. We don't trust one another. Were you ever able to rely on him? Don't you remember that time in the mountains when he left you hanging?

Judith He went to get the mountain rescue team!

Thomas Oh, come on! You couldn't go any further and he went on climbing without you.

Judith To call the mountain rescue team! And he was right. I had cramp in my arm. If he'd tried to help me –

Thomas He left you hanging there! Literally! Hanging!

Judith And that was the right thing to do!

Thomas If it had been the other way round, would you have done the same?

Judith If I had, it would have been the right thing to do.

Thomas But would you have done it?

Judith Of course.

Thomas He's hanging on the cliff face calling for help and you don't climb down to him, you keep going up? And you bring back the mountain rescue people nine hours later? Nine hours! You spent the whole night hanging on the cliff face and he was back at the hotel watching TV. Do you really believe you could have abandoned someone like that? That he won't say whatever he needs to say to save his skin? All we want from him is to hear him say it was your idea. That you forced him to take part. That's all we need. Then he can go home.

Judith You don't really think there's a bomb, do you? You're only saying you do so you can interrogate us without a lawyer.

Thomas If my ex-wife was in trouble, and she was told she could either save herself or me . . . I know what she would decide. And if I was in the same position, I know what I'd decide. And I really loved her. And she loved me. But people change. Time goes by. I can imagine why you got involved in all this nonsense. You wanted to prove you were still the person you used to be.

Judith Good God, it was an intellectual exercise! For my seminar.

Thomas You still think I'm an idiot.

Judith You're not an idiot. Everything you've been saying is reasonable. But it's on such a petty scale. It's such a narrow and cautious and dispirited reasonableness, which can't bear the idea of change and puts up with every bad situation because, you know, it could be worse.

That's what you're like. That's why they don't let you interrogate the dangerous terrorists, just . . . the ex-wife, the professor, in the next room.

Thomas And suppose something does get blown up – purely hypothetically – would that make everything better? Is that your . . . intellectual exercise?

Judith Blowing something up makes nothing at all better. But it is a symbol. The only sort everyone pays attention to. The shout with the furthest echo.

Pause.

Hence the intellectual exercise. In my seminar.

Thomas But no actual bomb?

Judith No.

Thomas Let's continue with your intellectual exercise, Professor. Your shout rings out. There are no fatalities, although there could have been, and for you that was an acceptable risk, but let's assume there aren't any. Then what?

Judith It's been twenty-four hours. You have to let Peter go. Otherwise you can't use what's in his statement.

Thomas You think he's made a statement?

Judith Not one that incriminates me.

Thomas You think he's that reliable? Remember. All those students. You knew about them, you loved him, and then you couldn't stand it any more.

Judith You think because he's the way he is, he'll say what you want to hear.

Thomas You're right, we will have to send him home soon. But you're staying here. He doesn't know what you're going to say in your statement. Not a happy thought for him. It'd really be in your interest –

Judith – to make a statement incriminating him. Sort of a pre-emptive strike.

Thomas You could call it that.

Judith A pre-emptive strike?

Thomas Yes.

Judith You want me to make something up?

Thomas Truth is a complicated concept. You know that better than anyone. Does a tree fall if no one sees it? 'Who's asking the question?'

Pause. He thinks for a moment.

Now I understand! If it's me who's asking, I'm imagining myself standing near the tree. By wanting to know about it, I've ensured it doesn't fall unobserved. Because I'm there. In my imagination. If it really fell without my imagining I was there, I wouldn't be asking the question. Is that what you meant?

Judith Do we really have time for this?

Thomas Not long ago my daughter said: 'What is it you do, Daddy? Are you a policeman?' 'In a way,' I said. 'But where's your uniform?' 'I don't have one,' I said. She was quite disappointed.

Judith You never really thought there was a bomb.

Thomas I always have to assume the worst. I always have to start out from the proposition that people are going to be killed.

Judith People are killed all the time and no one wants to know about it. Have you ever asked yourself why all the refugees who are pouring in here aren't more grateful? Aren't happy to be able to share all our values, aren't overwhelmed by our freedoms?

Thomas I feel sure you're about to explain it to me.

Judith Because they know what we don't want to know: that if you look at us from Africa, everything is a lie. For example: the principal export of a small country called Niger is uranium. European companies mine uranium in Niger, which means that in certain parts of the country, radiation levels are so high that the water is no longer drinkable. Pastureland becomes unusable, the desert expands and people have to migrate. They use up their last savings to get a place on a boat and, if they survive the crossing, they reach us. And because there isn't a war in Niger, we call them economic migrants.

Thomas And that justifies planting / a bomb?

Judith People die because of us every day and not in tens but thousands. Underneath our glass dome, humane values rule, but outside it what rules is chaos. The main threat to the world is not a few religious fanatics. The threat is hunger. The threat is poverty, as it always has been. And poverty isn't an accident. We create it. That's what's known as exploitation. And I've never said planting a bomb is justified.

Pause.

Thomas Why did you and Peter never have children?

Pause.

You did try. Medical procedures, I mean. An expensive process, not everyone can afford it, on top of which it doesn't always work; and now you're wondering how I know about it, despite the rules of medical confidentiality.

Judith I couldn't care less.

Thomas Among others, Ute, Karin, Marie, Inge, Ariane and all the recent students. They knew about it. They loved him. And for all your aversion to bourgeois values, at some point it got too much for you.

Judith He won't incriminate me and you don't have enough evidence.

Thomas All we have to say is, it was Christmas. Christmas! You think anyone will want to listen to what you have to say about uranium then? That you were thinking about a bomb outrage on *Christmas Day* – even if it was for your seminar, no one's going to like that. And what about Peter? He's left you in the lurch over and over again, any time he gets a chance, and you're still relying on him? Ute, Karin, Marie, Inge, Ariane. By the way, he did get Inge pregnant.

Judith has flinched and involuntarily covered her face with her hands. She tries not to let him notice, but without success. She trembles.

Of course he paid for the abortion. He even went with her when she had it. Like a gentleman.

Judith starts crying. She tries to suppress it but she's not able to, her whole body shudders with sobs. Thomas watches her, showing no sympathy.

Oh, come on. You haven't believed anything else I've said. Perhaps I made it up . . .

Long pause. Finally, she's able to calm down.

Judith All right.

Pause.

He didn't know anything about it. It was my laptop, it was my plan. The explosives were mine. I used his suitcase. That's my statement.

Thomas You're taking the rap?

Judith Now you have to let him go. You've held him for twenty-four hours without a lawyer.

Thomas Have you suddenly turned Christian? 'Greater love hath no man than this, that he lay down his life for his friends,' etc. Are you serious?

Judith You have to let him go.

Thomas Never mind explosives, you couldn't change a light bulb. You've never handled explosives. We can prove that.

Judith Gloves. Every time.

She reaches for a pencil and a piece of paper and starts writing.

It was my laptop, it was my plan. The explosives were mine. I used his suitcase.

Thomas Bullshit!

Judith You wanted me to incriminate him, didn't you? Not myself. Incriminating myself has ruined your whole strategy.

She hands him the piece of paper containing her confession. He accepts it, hesitatingly.

Thomas Take this bullshit back.

Judith Do you even have a daughter?

Thomas What sort of a question is that?

Judith Are you really divorced?

Thomas Why should I lie to you? We're never going to see each other again outside of this room.

Judith Why didn't it work between you and that poor woman who says you stole her youth away? Didn't you spend enough time at home? Did you work too hard,

39

were you married to your job? That's what people like you say, cliché-lovers: they like to say 'I was married to my job.'

Thomas There was another man. The love of her life. I was at best a passing fancy. Take back this ludicrous confession. The prosecutor will ask you for details, you'll start stuttering and the whole thing will collapse. The other way round is far more convincing. Peter was in charge of the bomb and you of the immortal prose.

Judith It was my laptop, it was my plan. The explosives were mine. I used his suitcase. He had nothing to do with it.

Thomas What about the bomb?

Judith I couldn't manage it. As you rightly said, I don't have the skills. It didn't work. But we live and learn. I'd have got there in the end.

Thomas Bullshit.

Pause.

Tell the truth. Say that Peter wanted to plant the bomb and you wanted to write the manifesto, because it was a way to preserve a connection with him and with your past and with the woman you used to be before it all fell apart and you were reduced to meeting, once a week in a hotel, out of sheer loneliness, that married idiot, quite ugly if you ask me, but that's your business, nothing to do with me. Perhaps Peter just took everything too literally. The whole thing got out of hand. Say that, it would help me. It would help you as well.

The phone rings, he picks up the receiver, listens for a while, hangs up and steps out of the room, leaving the door open. Judith, motionless, contemplates the open door. Some time passes. Eventually, he comes

*back. He slowly closes the door. He has a sheet of
paper in his hand.*

You knew, didn't you? You thought he wouldn't be able
to hold out.

Judith Has he . . . ?

Thomas reads aloud.

Thomas 'She was determined to plan an attack, I tried to
stop her, but once she gets something into her head, you
can't get through to her, I didn't know what to do.'

Judith He said that?

He hands her the piece of paper. She reads.

Thomas You saw this coming all along. You know him.
You know how weak he is. You knew he wouldn't go to
prison for you. But you didn't want to incriminate him,
so you could go free. That's why you incriminated
yourself, before he could . . . You're a very impressive
woman.

Judith Better to suffer injustice than to commit it.

Thomas Is that what Frantz-with-a-tz says?

Judith No, someone else.

Thomas You'll be asked to provide more detail.

Judith I have a very poor memory.

Thomas Where did you acquire the components?

Judith On the internet.

Thomas From where exactly?

Judith Can't remember.

Thomas What were the specific ingredients?

Judith Sorry, I've forgotten.

Thomas The instructions for assembling it?

Judith Internet.

Thomas Which website?

Judith I've forgotten.

Thomas Where are the materials now?

Judith I disposed of them.

Thomas Where?

Judith Landfill site.

Thomas Which one?

Judith Forgotten.

Thomas What was your target?

Judith I couldn't make up my mind. Possibly an empty department store, maybe a vacant ministry. Electricity pylons. I hadn't decided. I didn't want to kill anyone. Just do some damage, as much damage as possible, to some expensive property.

Thomas I don't understand.

Judith You've got everything you want. He took your offer and incriminated me, so you have to send him home. I've confessed. What more do you want?

Thomas I mean, I don't understand why you're doing this. Why you're taking this on yourself, just to protect this miserable bastard.

Judith I know you don't understand.

Thomas I wish my wife were like you.

Judith But I would never have been your wife.

Thomas Does he deserve this?

Judith What's it matter?

*There's a knock at the door. He goes over to the door
and opens it for a minute, somebody hands him a
handwritten piece of paper. He closes the door and
reads.*

Thomas Here.

Judith Sorry?

Thomas Your rights. You wanted them in writing.

He gives her the piece of paper.

Judith It's illegible.

Thomas I told you, the secretary is in Ibiza and my
colleague can't type.

Judith He can't type?

Thomas I know, amazing, isn't it? But people like that
still exist.

Judith It'll be twenty-four hours soon. You have to let
him go. He had a deal with you. If he incriminated me,
he'd go free. That's how our legal system works. If you
don't let him go right away as you promised, half of your
case collapses. His lawyer will see to that. He'll have a
good lawyer. And if his statement against me isn't
admissible, because you kept him here too long without a
lawyer and violated the deal, I'll withdraw my confession
and you'll have nothing.

Thomas We're not amateurs. We threw him out the
minute he'd signed his statement. We didn't even let him
finish his coffee. So, the two of us? We'd better call your
parents after all.

Judith Looks like it.

43

Thomas Your choice.

Judith You know, I really don't like that dog much.

Thomas Henry.

He smiles, and for a second she smiles as well.

Suppose we'd got to know each other under different circumstances.

Judith Yes?

Thomas Would you have found me just as unsympathetic?

Judith What circumstances did you have in mind?

Thomas I don't know. On the tube. In a train. I could have sat next to you on a plane.

Judith Flying where?

Thomas To Italy, for example. For a holiday.

Judith I don't take holidays in Italy.

Thomas It was just an example.

Judith I tend to fly to conferences. In Princeton or Geneva. Or Bordeaux. Ever go to Geneva?

Thomas Hardly ever.

Judith I take my holidays in Switzerland. Or California. You often in California?

Thomas says nothing.

You see!

Thomas There's lots of places we could have . . .

Judith You think so?

Thomas Doesn't matter where.

Judith But it does matter where. I wouldn't think we have any friends in common.

Thomas I could have been sitting next to you, on a train, let's say –

Judith Do you travel first class?

Thomas No.

Judith I do.

Thomas The air-conditioning fails in first class, so you move back to second. We fall into conversation. I don't share your opinions, but my point of view is not completely uninteresting. We talk, time passes. We talk about structural violence. And whether a tree is really there. And so on. Might happen.

Judith And I think to myself, what an interesting man.

Thomas Something like that.

Judith Someone you can have a real discussion with.

Thomas Yes.

Judith And we could have said: 'Let's continue this conversation. Let's meet up. Let's have a coffee and pick up where we left off.'

Thomas And in these different circumstances . . . I'd just like to know. As we're speaking so frankly.

Judith Are you allowed to ask me questions like this?

Thomas That's why we're here, for me to ask questions.

Judith looks at the mirror.

Judith Is anyone watching us?

Thomas Normally, there'd be half a dozen of us sitting behind the mirror, eating doughnuts, but it's Christmas.

Judith Are we being recorded?

Thomas No.

Judith No?

Thomas It's bust.

Judith What?

Thomas Christmas Eve, no technicians in the building. We're not as well-organised as people think. We can call out the emergency forces in about an hour, our helicopters are on permanent standby, but the IT staff are on a different contract, which says: holidays are holidays. Anyway, to get back to what we were saying. If we'd met under different circumstances . . . As we're speaking frankly.

Judith You want me to speak frankly?

Thomas Yes.

Judith One look at your face would have been enough.

　Pause.

Thomas I see.

Judith I would have taken one look at your face and known everything. If, in spite of that, I'd been obliged to speak to you, I'd have put as quick a stop to it as possible. And if I hadn't been able to put a quick stop to it, I'd have run away. Except, of course, you'd have locked the door. Was that sufficiently frank?

Thomas We have everything we need. Your ex-husband has incriminated you, we have the text from your laptop. A profile is emerging. And personally, yes, I've always thought it rather unlikely that the two of you built the bomb together. You're not someone I can take seriously. You were always solitary. Never more solitary than with this man, to whom at some point you decided to commit yourself, without his ever really committing himself to you, and for whom you've sacrificed everything, without his ever having sacrificed anything for you. Your future is now behind you, you've nothing left to hope for and that's precisely why you would have tried something at some point, perhaps even a bombing, had we not intervened in time. Yes, Professor, perhaps now's the time to call your lawyer.

Judith Where am I going to find a lawyer on Christmas Eve? As you explained to me, my lawyer is in Iceland.

Thomas Yes, that could be a problem. Especially as you're only allowed one phone call.

Judith Can I make the call now?

Thomas In a couple of days, when the holidays are over, we'll call a press conference. We'll show them your photo and a picture of your house, although it has nothing to do with anything; but it's now become an established practice always to show a picture of the house. That's where they had their meetings, we'll say. That's where it all happened.

Judith Can I make my call now?

He pushes the phone over to her. She picks up the receiver and dials a number she knows by heart.

It's me . . . Yes. I understand. Me too.

She hangs up.

Thomas Was that him?

Judith Yes.

Thomas You used your only call to ring up a man who's just . . . !

Judith Yes.

Thomas That was the only call you're allowed.

Judith I know.

Thomas You won't get another one.

Thomas stares at her for a moment, then grabs the phone back and presses the redial button. He listens: no answer. He hangs up and hastily dials another number.

(*Into phone.*) Re-arrest him, now!

Judith That time on the cliff-face. I could have died. There all night. The idea of falling is so tempting. It's true what they say. If you spend long enough on the edge of an abyss, you want to go over.

Thomas (*into phone*) What do you mean, you've lost him? What do you mean, you've lost him? Then locate his phone!

He hangs up.

Judith Didn't you say you didn't think there was one?

The phone rings. Thomas picks up the receiver, listens, replaces it. He's stunned, panicking.

He threw the phone away, didn't he?

Thomas Why?

Judith There's no law against it.

Thomas Why would he throw his phone away?

Judith Throwing a phone away isn't illegal.

Thomas There is no bomb! People like you couldn't plant a bomb.

Judith Couldn't we?

Thomas You said yourself it's not right to plant bombs.

Judith Sometimes it might be better to do something wrong than nothing at all.

The phone rings.

Thomas Nothing's going to happen, nothing! Nothing at all!

Judith is very calm now, she's more speaking to herself than him.

Judith That time in Chile. They interrogated us in separate cells. We both confessed. We incriminated one another. I would have said anything to get out of there. There wasn't much to confess, a few pamphlets, a smuggled gun. We promised each other that nothing like that would ever happen again. Whatever happened between us. Never again. Sometimes you have to take a decision . . . on behalf of someone else. Sometimes you have to decide in someone else's favour.

Thomas And that's what you've done?

Judith That's what we've done.

Thomas looks at the clock. Judith looks at the clock. At the instant the hands reach midnight, there's a blackout.